River Otters

Aquatic Clowns!

Dr. Richard A. NeSmith

Love of Nature Series

ISSUE 8

Applied Principles of Education & Learning

APE-Learning

© 2020 Richard A. NeSmith
Love of Nature Series

All Rights Reserved.

No part of this book may be reproduced, transmitted, or stored in any form or by any means except for your own personal use without the express, written permission of the author. All graphs, drawings, and charts are created by the author or utilize public illustrations according to fair use for teaching, research, scholarship, and reporting. Some photos are those of the author's, and some are creative commons licensed. Special thanks to the following who contributed pro-bono from their collections.[i] Thank you all.

This book contains material used under the "Fair Use" of copyrighted material as provided for in section 107 of the US Copyright Law.

dr.nesmith@gmail.com

http://richardnesmith.obior.cc

All images in this book are copyright by their respective authors.

Dr. Richard A. NeSmith
Winter Haven, FL 33884

dr.nesmith@gmail.com

Oct 2021

ISBN: 9798674450474

FLESCH-KINCAID GRADE LEVEL: 8.8

River Otters
(Lontra *canadensis*)

River otters are called many things. Water sausages! Silky swimmers! And cheeky water pups or water cats! We have called them *Aquatic Clowns* because of their love of fun, curiosity, and utter playfulness. Otters might be the most fun-loving, majestic mammals in North America. *Lontra* is the Latin word for "otter," and *canadensis* means "of Canada." The word *otter* is an *Old English* word meaning "water animal." There are seven subspecies of Lontra *canadensis*.

River otters are related to weasels, minks, ferrets, badgers, and wolverines. They are cousins to the larger sea otters.[1]

---

[1] Sea otters are from an entirely different genus-species (Enhydra *lutris*) and do not interbreed.

RIVER OTTERS: *AQUATIC CLOWNS!*

They are best known for their playfulness and sense of curiosity. Playing together helps keep family bonds secure, and teaches the babies (pups or kittens) necessary hunting, forging, and scent-marking skills. Mothers will catch and release prey to teach their young how to forage and to find food items.

River otters are very social creatures and want attention, sometimes even demanding it. Some have also suggested that otters might be some of the smartest animals on the planet. We will see how vital otters are to the ecosystem.

Range

From a family called Mustelids, these semi-aquatic mammals are found in nearly every region throughout North America, with a river system or large lakes. The river otter population is currently 100,000, with over 4,000 otters reintroduced in 21 states since 1976.

River otters do not live in northern Canada, southern California, or the Mohave Desert, extending into southern Nevada and western Arizona. Neither are they found in the dry arid regions of New Mexico, Texas, and Colorado. There are other isolated regions or portions of their range where humans locally eliminated otters. Unfortunately, this practice is still done unofficially in some areas as they see the otter as a threat to "fishing." Re-establishment and protection efforts have helped stabilize some populations.

A North American river otter's home range can be as broad as 30 square miles (78 square kilometers). However, the typical territory is 3 to 15 square miles (4.8 to 24 square

km.).

Characteristics

River otters spend part of their time in water (semiaquatic). They have long, slender streamline bodies, and have short, powerful legs, five toes, sharp claws, and webbed-feet. They have a tapered tail (acting somewhat like a rudder) that can be one-third of its body length. River otters have rounded heads with small ears and nostrils (of which both can be closed upon diving underwater).

They can grow to be more than 3.3 feet (1 meter) long, from head to tail, and weigh up to 30-40 pounds (14-18 kg). Males are larger than females. The coat is water-repellant due to a specialized gland that secretes oil. Their oily fur is unique, dense, lustrous, durable, soft, and was much sought after by early American trappers. Their fur is said to be the thickest of any animal, with 850,000 to one million hairs per square inch. The density increases its temperature insulation, along with stored body fat protecting them in cold water.

The fur is dark brown to black on the back and a lighter color on the belly. The throat and cheeks are usually golden-brown. In the late 1970s, the annual harvest in North America of river otter pelts reached approximately 50,000, with a value of US$3 million.

As river otters spend much of their lives underwater, it is not very useful, depending on sight or sound. However, they have other sensory receptors that do assist them, whiskers, known as *vibrissae*. These are long and thick stiff hairs growing around the mouth. They are vital sensory organs that permit the animal to touch, smell, and identify food or predators underwater. These whiskers are particularly useful when foraging for food in murky waters.

All river otters have scent glands. These glands assist otters in marking off their territory, thus family name Mustelids. River otters are fast, agile, *unmatched* swimmers (up to 6-7 mph/10 kph). M*ustelids*, including otters, have powerful jaws and specialized sharp teeth, including ripping canines and large cheek teeth (called carnassials). Both of these types of teeth are for inflicting lethal bites and tearing off flesh. North American river otters also have large molars.

RIVER OTTERS: *AQUATIC CLOWNS!*

Molars can crush hard objects like the shells of mollusks. An adult North American river otter has 36 teeth, but additional premolars may be present. River otters chew their food quite thoroughly and leave very little waste behind. River otters wash themselves clean after every meal.

River otters are near the top of the food chain. However, they do have predators. They have few natural predators when they are in the water (namely, alligators and

RIVER OTTERS: *AQUATIC CLOWNS!*

crocodiles). Otters mainly escape predation through their quickness in the water and on land. They are watchful and are fiercely able to defend themselves and their young. There are reports of river otters attacking and drowning dogs.

The most significant of the river otter fatalities seem to be the automobiles, habitat loss, and pollution. Regulations and strategies, however, seem to have stopped current threats to continuing otter populations. However, humans now remain the most significant threat for otters, not from hunting but human wetlands development.

Natural land predators include bobcats, lynxes, wolves, raptors, coyotes, foxes, mountain lions, black bears, and domestic dogs. Otters do well defending themselves, though they prefer to avoid confrontation. When cornered on land, they will fight and scratch. The most susceptible to predators is the young river otters. In the wild, river otters live less than ten years. In captivity, they can live 10-15 years.

RIVER OTTERS: *AQUATIC CLOWNS!*

The very nature of the river otter makes it stand out among most animals. They appear very charismatic, witty and display charming liveliness. In addition, they are highly playful, frisky, spirited, and lively creatures. Everyday river otter playtime activities are amusing, if not unusual, to watch. These include somersaulting, wrestling, flopping around, and sliding. Also, they cuddle and groom and chase one another.

A river otter's sense of smell and hearing abilities are keen. So is their sense of touch in their paws. However, their eyesight is not very good, and they are quite near-sighted. As a result, they are unable to see things clearly unless they are relatively close. So, there are times when a river otter might walk up to something or someone before realizing what they are encountering. The sight issue is a consequence of being able to see above and underwater.

River otters are adaptive swimmers. They have an extra set of transparent eyelids that act like swimming goggles. Also, river otters have two lungs, but the right lung is larger than the left. This lung difference possibly enhances holding one's breath for more extended periods. Finally, the length of the river otter's trachea is in-between the size compared to that of the terrestrial carnivores and marine mammals. The shorter trachea may improve air exchange and increases lung ventilation in diving mammals.

Diet

Otters are expert hunters and foragers but also opportunistic predators (eating what is most convenient). River otters are *omnivores* and eat a variety of aquatic wildlife and plants. Their diet includes fish (perch seems to be their favorite), crayfish, crabs, snails, mussels, and worms, amphibians (frogs and salamanders). They also eat small insects, bird eggs, birds, reptiles (snakes and turtles), and small mammals, such as mice, muskrats, rabbits, and even immature beavers. River otters have a very high metabolism, so *they need to eat frequently.*

The river otter's food web includes the vast biodiversity of life. Remove it from the ecosystem, and many animals are affected. From the diagram, one can see the complexities that exist between predator and prey.

Habitat

We have seen the river otters' range, which is vast, and nearly any region with adequate river and lake systems where there are permanent food supplies. River otters live in freshwater and coastal marine habitats, including rivers, lakes, marshes, swamps, and estuaries.

River otters can tolerate a variety of environments, including cold and warmer latitudes and high elevations. North American river otters, however, do seem to be very sensitive to pollution and disappear from areas with unclean waters. This sensitivity may be that they readily accumulate high levels of mercury, pesticides, and other chemical elements in their bodies. River otters are, therefore, *bioindicators* of healthy aquatic environments.

River otters are considered *keystone* species. They significantly modify their habitat, but not to the extinct that a beaver might. First, their presence regulates species lower in the food chain and influences the water-to-land nutrient transport. Secondly, by contributing to primary production (plant growth), river otters increase the occurrence and growth in the surrounding *riparian* (riverbank) habitat. Finally, their scat and urine latrines change the chemical composition, adding additional nitrogen to the ground. These aspects do change the environment and plant growth due to their presence.

Though spending a great deal of time in the water, the river otter *lives* on land, building dens in the burrows provided by other animals (former beaver or nutria dens), in natural hollows (such as could be found under a fallen log, or burrowed in river banks). Often these dens have underwater entrances with one or more tunnels leading to a chamber lined with grass, leaves, moss, bark, and hair. Tunnels provide easy access to water. This interaction between land and water only reemphasizes why otters live along rivers, bogs, and various waterways.

Behavior

A family of otters is called a *romp*. It can also be called a bevy, family, or lodge. They are primarily solitary (living alone). However, the females frequently are accompanied by their young (though ignored or tolerated by the male). The young stay with mom for about a year until the next pups are born. River otters, especially the mothers, are very territorial but often try to avoid others. They defend their territory by marking, scratching, and at times, fighting.

River otters do not hibernate and are active year-round. But as temperatures rise, they become more nocturnal (active at night) but diurnal (busy during the day) during winter. They are most interactive with the environment during dusk and dawn (*crepuscular*). They prefer to stay in a general region and not considered migratory. But do travel based on food supply and shortages or environmental conditions (such as pollution). They tend to settle in areas that have ample vegetation, rock piles, and adequate coverage.

Though North American river otters spend two-thirds of their time on land, they are tremendous swimmers. They are not the *dog paddlers* we often see in many swimming animals. Instead, their swimming skills are coordinated and specialized for the task at hand. They gracefully swim with all four limbs (*quadrupedal paddling*) and alternate with forelimb and hind limb paddling. The tail is round, plump, and more abundant in surface area than its legs and provides a means of both stability and short bursts of swift force and propulsion. They can hold their breath for up to 8 minutes underwater and dive to a depth of 60 feet (18.3 meters).

While swimming at the surface, the dorsal (back) of the river otter's head maintains the eyes, ears, and nostrils exposed above the water level. It must, however, continue

its forward motion to support this beneficial position.

River otters also move quite swiftly on land, up to 29 miles per hour (47 kph). They travel by walking, running, leaping, and sliding. They enjoy sliding across ice and snow or even down grassy slopes and muddy banks. This is a very energy-efficient means of traveling, which they enjoy.

Reproduction

River otter mating season is in late winter or early spring. Boars (males) mate with sows (females) during this time, though each might mate with more than one partner throughout their lives. The male, however, will leave the female to do the raising of the otter pups. Thus, a *family unit* will consist of only the mother and her young. On occasions, other adult female otters might join the family unit as

helpers.

Gestation (the period of pregnancy) lasts for 60-63 days. A litter will number from one to six pups per year, with an average being 2 to 3. Otters are born with fur but otherwise are helpless and entirely dependent on their mother. Birth, nursing, and caring for the young occur in the den near water. At about three months old, the young pups wean.

Mother otters will care for their young juvenile, growing fast and leaving her care at six months old. The young pups then begin to scatter by the time the sow gives birth again. Pups reach sexual maturity around the age of 2 to 3 years of age, though river otters don't breed until they are at least five years old.

Another unique characteristic of the otter, like that of the armadillo, is the ability to delay reproductive fertilization. In other words, otter sows can withhold her fertilized egg implantation so that it will not implant in her uterus for several months.

Miscellaneous

It seems that river otters have boundless energy due to their very high metabolism. Such liveliness requires that they eat frequently and eat a lot during the day.

The otter itself is relatively clean and well-groomed. However, they have particularly stinky poop (feces), which even has its own unique name: *spraints*. They also produce a pungent, disagreeable scent from their anal glands. It is believed these strong odors, which some scientists describe as smelling like violets, probably occur from the otter's seafood/fish diet.

The North American river otter is susceptible to disease and parasites. These include canine distemper, rabies, respiratory and urinary infections. Alone with various common worms (nematodes, trematodes, and cestodes). Ectoparasites (those external on the body) include ticks, sucking lice, and fleas.

The United States Forest Service has designated river otters as a "sensitive species." They want to continue monitoring them and tracking possible pollutants that would significantly reduce their population. There are laws protecting river otters in Colorado, Kansas, Nebraska, South Dakota, and Wyoming. Trapping is allowed in some states.

River otters are possibly the funniest and most animated animals to watch. They appear to be curious but fun-loving. How much of this is true might be in our human personification of these creatures. Like all wild animals, they have a vicious side to them, and they can be brutal in their survival role. But, these animals are so loved, such

negative views are either ignored or rarely reported, such as one leaping on a female kayaker's face.

RIVER OTTERS: *AQUATIC CLOWNS!*

In closing, river otters are fun and entertaining creatures to watch. *They cause us to laugh and smile and sometimes to realize that we need to enjoy our environments around us.* This we have learned from these *aquatic clowns!*

RIVER OTTERS: *AQUATIC CLOWNS!*

REVIEW

1. What time of day are river otters most active?

2. What prevents an otter from getting too cold when swimming in cold water?

3. List one disease to which river otters are susceptible?

4. Where does the mother river otter raise her newborns?

5. How long does the average river otter live?

6. List two traits that help the river otter be an outstanding swimmer.

RIVER OTTER

COLORING PAGE

http://www.supercoloring.com/coloring-pages/realistic-river-otter

RIVER OTTERS: *AQUATIC CLOWNS!*

Name:_____

River Otters: Aquatic Clowns!
Carefully read each statement or clue, then fill in the letters in the appropriate squares.

Created using the Crossword Maker on TheTeachersCorner.net

vibrissae   weasels   perch   closes   territory   sea   kittens   pollution   habitat   water

metabolism   webbed   population   desert   wash

Across
1. River otter's favorite food?
6. River otters are closely related to _____.
8. Larger cousin of the river otter is the ____ otter?
9. The word otter is an Old English word meaning "_____ animal."
10. The river otter _____ is 100,000.
13. River otter's whiskers?

Down
2. That which most threatens river otters today is _____ loss?
3. Unique feature about river otter's head, ears, and nostril during diving?
4. River otters are very sensitive to _____.
5. A typical otter _____ is 3 to 15 square miles
6. _____ feet help otters to be great swimmers
7. Because of the river otters high _____ they must eat often.
9. After every meal, river otters _____ themselves.
11. Baby river otters are called pups or _____.
12. One place you will NOT find a river otter?

27

INTERESTING SOURCES TO CONSIDER

Back from the Brink: The North American River Otter. Available at: https://youtu.be/PcI1Wynq--w

Day 3 - North American River Otters. Available at: https://youtu.be/oQcA188ENks

Facts about Otters. Live Science. Available at: https://www.livescience.com/55090-otter-facts.html

NatureMapping Animal Facts for Kids: River Otters. Available at: http://naturemappingfoundation.org/natmap/facts/river_otter_k6.html

North American River Otter. Smithsonian's National Zoo & Conservation Biology Institute. Available at: https://nationalzoo.si.edu/animals/north-american-river-otter

North American River Otter. BioKids. Available at: http://www.biokids.umich.edu/critters/Lontra_canadensis/
North American River Otters. #WildWednesday. Available at: https://youtu.be/0w7VCzqsSCo

North American River Otters. National Geographic. Available at: https://www.nationalgeographic.com/animals/mammals/n/north-american-river-otter/

River Otter Facts. Available at: https://facts.net/nature/animals/river-otter-facts

River Otters: National Geographic Kids. Available at: https://kids.nationalgeographic.com/animals/mammals/river-otter/

Seven Quick Facts About River Otters. National Forest Foundation. https://www.nationalforests.org/blog/seven-quick-facts-about-river-otters

Top 20 Amazing Facts about North American River Otters. Available at: https://youtu.be/Zj6cny3Ei0c

ABOUT THE AUTHOR

Richard NeSmith is a native of Florida, USA. He grew up wading through the swamps of central Florida with his two younger brothers during the pre-Disney era and unknowingly, falling in love with biology, wildlife, and nature. He has lived in seven American states, twice in Australia and once in Mexico City. He holds eight university degrees and has taught for 14 years in secondary schools, here and abroad, and another 13 years as a professor in several American universities. His service includes professor of science education, Dean of Education, Campus Dean, and an online instructor. His passion for learning (and *how we learn*) did not develop until *after* graduating from high school. His only explanation for this is that *having a goal made all the difference in the world*. He enjoys reading, hiking, nature photography, golf, and tennis.

http://richardnesmith.obior.cc

Applied **P**rinciples of **E**ducation & Learning
presents

APE-Learning

AMAZON AUTHOR's PAGE:
https://www.amazon.com/author/richardnesmith

Educational, wildlife, and naturalist books available by Dr. Richard NeSmith.

RIVER OTTERS: *AQUATIC CLOWNS!*

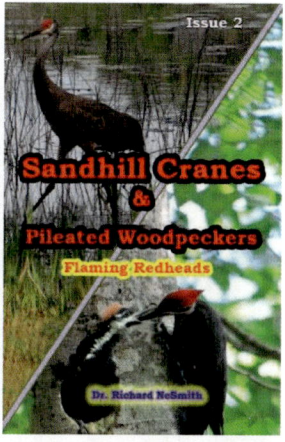

RIVER OTTERS: *AQUATIC CLOWNS!*

RIVER OTTERS: *AQUATIC CLOWNS!*

[i] Special thanks to the following who kindly provided permission to use their photographs. From Pixabay: Dušan Smetana, mitzy123, Sendy Wulandhary, Katie Henthorn, Skeeze, Christian Deckmann, Sendy Wulandhary, hamikus, Julian Gough, Richard John, Vinson Tan, Ian Lindsay, Nimpus.

In addition, *special thanks* to fellow nature lovers: **Deborah L. Blic, Stacey Diamond, Rosemary Crosman, Phil Stone, Pam Maniec, Wendy Lund,** and **Greg Jowers** for wonderful photos. And, as always, special thanks to **Dr. Laurie Aleixo**, for her photographs, her rehab work, and her support and encouragement. ***Thank you all.***

Made in the USA
Las Vegas, NV
26 April 2024

89197005R00021